The Civil War

Written by Jason Hook
Illustrated by David McAllister

What were the two sides in the Civil War?

AMERICAN FOUGHT AGAINST AMERICAN. ON ONE SIDE were the North, or Union forces, who represented the 23 northern states of the elected government. On the other were the forces of the South, or Confederacy, who fought for the 11 Southern states. These rebel states had broken away from the Union, and elected their own president.

What did Walt Whitman say about the Civil War?

The famous poet called it that "strange, sad war." His phrase described the nature of the war perfectly. It was a war in which brother fought against brother, and a nation slaughtered its own finest men. Whitman witnessed the conflict firsthand as a volunteer in a military hospital. He also wrote: "Future years will never know the seething hell and black infernal background, and it is best they should not."

Where did the fighting take place?

The war was divided into two main areas by the Appalachian Mountains. East to the Atlantic, most battles took place in Virginia between the two capitals Washington and Richmond. To the west, the two sides fought for control of the Mississippi River. The North also blockaded the South's coast with ships in the Atlantic, and Gulf of Mexico.

Which states were in the Union?

California, Connecticut, Delaware, Illinois, Indiana, Iowa, Kansas, Kentucky, Maine, Maryland, Massachusetts, Michigan, Minnesota, Missouri, New Hampshire, New Jersey, New York, Ohio, Oregon, Pennsylvania, Rhode Island, Vermont, and Wisconsin. In addition, the "organized territories" of Colorado, Dakota, Nebraska, Nevada, New Mexico, Utah, and Washington wished to join the Union as free states.

Which states were in the Confederacy?

Alabama, Arkansas, Florida, Georgia, Louisiana, Mississippi, North and South Carolina, Tennessee, Texas, and Virginia. There were also some "border states." Rebel governments in Kentucky and Missouri supported the South.

Union
soldier

Abraham
Lincoln

Which was the only state ever to have two presidents?

Kentucky. The President of the Union, Abraham Lincoln, and the
President of the Confederacy, Jefferson Davis, were both born in
Kentucky, near the Ohio River.

How many people supported the opposing sides?

The South had a population of about 9 million people. Of these, more
than 3 million were black slaves. The North found volunteers for its
army in a much larger population of more than 22 million.

Which side had the most money?

The North was the center of America's big cities, industries,
commerce, factories, and railroads. It boasted 75 percent of the
nation's wealth. The poorer South wished to preserve its traditional
world of cotton plantations worked by slaves.

What kind of war was it?

The Civil War is often described as the first "modern" war. Many
modern weapons were first used in this conflict, yet the tactics
were very old-fashioned. The combined result created
very high casualties.

When was the Civil War?

CONFEDERATE FORCES FIRST OPENED
FIRE AT FORT SUMTER, CHARLESTON,
on April 12, 1861. Four years later, almost exactly, the
main Confederate forces under General Robert E. Lee
surrendered at Appomattox on April 9, 1865. The last
Confederates surrendered on May 26.

5

John Brown was the leader
of the abolitionists.

Who lived in *Uncle Tom's Cabin*?

A character in the novel of that name, written in 1852 by Harriet Beecher Stowe. Her sentimental story described the evils of slavery, which was an accepted practice in the Southern states. It sold 300,000 copies in its first year. The novel, and plays based on it, converted many people in the North into "abolitionists" who wished to ban slavery. It outraged many Southerners, who saw the novel as an attack on their way of life.

What was the Missouri Compromise of 1820?

In 1819, there were 11 "slave" and 11 "free" states. To preserve this balance, when the slave state of Missouri joined the Union in 1820, Maine joined as a free state. The government agreed that no new slave states north of Missouri would be admitted to the Union. For the first time, the Union had been divided into North and South.

Why do people sing about John Brown?

On October 16, 1859, fanatical abolitionist John Brown led a raid on the armory at Harper's Ferry, Virginia. He planned to steal enough weapons to lead a slave uprising in Virginia. His plan was foiled by U.S. Marines, and Brown was hanged in December. The soldiers of the North remembered Brown when they marched to war singing: "John Brown's body lies a'moldering in the grave."

Who was "Moses"?

THIS WAS THE NAME SLAVES GAVE TO HARRIET TUBMAN. AFTER ESCAPING slavery in 1849, she returned south 18 times to lead over 300 slaves to freedom. She was part of the "Underground Railroad," the secret organization that led slaves to freedom in the North.

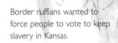

Border ruffians wanted to force people to vote to keep slavery in Kansas.

How many black slaves were there?

There were over 3 million black slaves on the cotton plantations of the South. Slaves were recognized as property in the U.S. Constitution.

What was the Fugitive Slave Law?

A law passed as part of a new "compromise" in 1850. To keep the South happy, the law made it possible to return runaway slaves in the North to their owners. It created fury in the North. Poet Ralph Waldo Emerson called it "a filthy law."

Who smashed his cane over someone's head in the Senate?

Preston Brooks, Representative of South Carolina, beat unconscious Senator Charles Sumner, who had given a speech denouncing supporters of slavery. Brooks wrote: "The fragments of the stick are begged for as sacred relics."

Why was Abraham Lincoln elected President in 1860?

Lincoln's Republican Party, formed in 1854, was elected because the vote for the Democratic Party was split between two candidates. Lincoln became President without winning a single Southern state, many of whom refused to put his name on the poll.

Which state was the first to leave the Union?

South Carolina, which declared the Union "dissolved" on December 20, 1861. The other slave states soon followed, and on February 8 declared a new nation named the Confederate States of America.

Who were the "Border Ruffians"?

IN 1854, IT WAS DECIDED THAT THE INHABITANTS OF THE NEW territory of Kansas could vote on being a slave state or a free state. Pro-slavery gangs who rushed from Missouri to Kansas to cast illegal votes and to attack abolitionist voters were called "Border Ruffians."

7

Who was Abraham Lincoln?

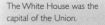

The White House was the capital of the Union.

Lincoln was President and Commander-in-Chief

of the North's forces. He was a striking figure, 6 ft 4 in (1.9 m) tall and a brilliant speaker. Lincoln had little military experience, but turned out to be a good commander. On March 4, 1861, he traveled to his inauguration in secret because of an assassination plot. In his speech he said: "In your hands, my dissatisfied fellow countrymen, and not in mine, is the momentous issue of civil war."

General McClellan

Who was General Ulysses S. Grant?

Grant was the victorious commander of the North's troops at the end of the war. He had become a hero in 1862 when he demanded unconditional surrender from a Confederate general. Supporters said his initials stood for "Unconditional Surrender," and sent him so many cigars that he gave up his pipe. When prohibitionists complained that Grant drank heavily, Lincoln replied: "What brand does he drink? I'd like to send a barrel of it to the other generals."

Who were the Graybeards?

The Graybeard Regiment were all aged 45 and over. Other regiments fighting for the North were also given nicknames: Perry's Saints (all officers were ministers); La Garde Lafayette (French New Yorkers); Teacher's Regiment (mainly college professors); and Temperance Regiment (did not drink alcohol).

Who was George B. McClellan?

McClellan was commander of the North's troops in the early part of the war. His cautiousness infuriated Lincoln. When he complained about fatigued horses, Lincoln wrote: "Will you pardon me for asking what the horses of your army have done ... that could fatigue anything?"

Where was the capital of the Union?

Stars and Stripes

It REMAINED IN WASHINGTON, WITHIN THE SLAVE STATE OF VIRGINIA. FROM the White House window, Lincoln could watch Confederate forces gathering. Until 10,000 Union troops arrived in May 1861, there was a danger that Washington would be captured.

Which songs did the North sing?
Their songs included *Yankee Doodle, We'll Rally Round the Flag,* and *The Girl I Left Behind Me. The Battle Hymn of the Republic* and *John Brown's Body* were both sung to a tune that actually came from the South.

What names were given to the Union forces?
They were known as the Union, the Federal Army, the Republic, the North, the Yanks or Yankees, and the Blues. Confederate soldiers nicknamed the Union soldiers "Billy Yank."

What flag did the North fight under?
The Stars and Stripes. War broke out when the South bombarded Fort Sumter, South Carolina, which was flying the American flag. After surrendering, the fort commander took the tattered flag away with him. He returned to rehoist the same flag four years later.

What was a black sentry supposed to have told Ulysses S. Grant?
On seeing an officer walk past smoking, the sentry is famously supposed to have said: "You must throw away that cigar, sir!"

9

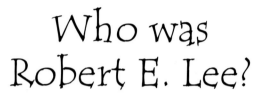

Who was Robert E. Lee?

LEE WAS THE GREATEST SOLDIER OF THE CIVIL WAR. HIS FIRST LINK TO the Civil War was when he commanded the Marines who arrested John Brown at Harper's Ferry. When the war broke out, he was offered command of the North's forces, but declined through loyalty to his home state of Virginia. He took command of the South's forces in 1862 and proved himself to be a daring and brilliant commander. His soldiers were devoted to him and named him "Marse Lee."

Who was Jefferson Davis?

Davis took the oath as President of the Confederacy on February 18, 1861. A graduate of West Point and an experienced soldier, he would have preferred a commission in the army. Just as Lee was not a supporter of slavery, so Davis was famous for his kindness to his slaves. He was imprisoned for two years after the war for treason. Seven Southern states still celebrate a legal holiday on his birthday, June 3.

How many horses were shot from under Nathan Bedford Forrest?

Forrest had 29 horses shot from under him during the war, and was frequently injured. He was a brilliant cavalry commander for the South who started the war as a private and progressed to major general. Sherman called him "the very Devil."

Was Robert E. Lee born to be a soldier?

Yes. Lee came from a famous military family. His father, Henry "Light Horse Harry" Lee, was George Washington's favorite cavalry commander. He also had ancestors who had fought with William the Conqueror and in the Crusades.

Who were the Yankee Hunters?

The Barbour County Yankee Hunters was the nickname of one of the Confederates' units. Others were the Cherokee Lincoln Killers, Hornet's Nest Riflemen, and Tallapossa Thrashers.

Robert E. Lee

Stars and Bars

Battle flag

Why did the South have two flags?

What songs did the Confederates sing?

Their songs included *The Yellow Rose of Texas* and *The Bonnie Blue Flag*. The most famous song of the South, *Dixie*, was actually written in the North by the son of an abolitionist.

How big was the South's army?

At the start of the war, the Confederates created a regular army of 10,000 soldiers. In America, though, the tradition was for civilian volunteers to fight. In all, some one million men fought for the South.

THE OFFICIAL CONFEDERATE FLAG, THE STARS AND BARS, WAS VERY SIMILAR to the Stars and Stripes. So, a red "battle flag" with stars on a blue saltire (diagonal cross) was also used. The first ones were made from silk intended for ladies' dresses.

What names were given to the Confederate forces?

They were known as the Confederates, the South, the Rebels, and the Grays. Union soldiers nicknamed their Confederate enemy "Johnny Reb."

Where was the capital of the Confederacy?

At Richmond, just 103 miles (166 km) south of Washington. When the North learned that the Confederate Congress would meet there in July 1861, the New York Tribune started a famous warcry: "Forward to Richmond! Forward to Richmond!"

The ruins of the arsenal at Richmond.

Did any women sign up to fight?

Up to 400 women disguised themselves as men so that they could enlist. They were able to do this because the doctors who examined new recruits barely looked at them. One famous soldier was Jennie Hodgers, an Irishwoman who joined the 95th Illinois Volunteers under the name of Albert Cashier. She remained undiscovered throughout the war, fighting in several major battles and receiving a pension after the armistice.

Could people avoid conscription?

Rich people on both sides could pay for a "substitute" to fight in their place. This might cost a Southern farmer up to $6,000. The arrival of unfit substitutes horrified professional soldiers. One substitute was said to have been lured from an asylum.

Did families fight on the same side?

No, the tragedy of the war was that it tore families apart. William and James Terrill were brothers who fought on opposite sides. Both rose to the rank of brigadier general and both were killed. President Lincoln's wife Mary had three half brothers who died fighting for the South.

A few women joined the army by pretending to be men.

How old were the soldiers?

ALL AGES. CURTIS KING ENLISTED IN IOWA'S "GRAYBEARDS" regiment at the ripe old age of 80. The most famous youngster in the war was Johnny Clem, the "Drummer Boy of Chickamauga." He enlisted age nine. At Chickamauga he used a sawn-off musket to shoot a Confederate officer who had shouted at him: "Surrender you little Yankee devil!" When he retired in 1915 as Major General Clem, he was the last active soldier left from the war.

Were all the soldiers American?

Were all the soldiers white?
The Union refused to use black soldiers until 1862. After this date, nearly 180,000 black soldiers fought, and 21 were awarded the Medal of Honor. Not surprisingly, black soldiers served for the South only as servants and musicians.

N O, THEY INCLUDED ENGLISH, French, Dutch, and Hungarian soldiers, and a Scottish regiment that fought in kilts. One man listed his nationality simply as "the ocean." Native American names on the lists include Big Mush, John Bearmeat, and Warkiller Hogshooter.

Drummer boy

What did the soldiers do before the war?
The North boasted soldiers from an enormous variety of occupations, and official lists of soldiers' jobs include Paper Hanger, Gambler, Sugar Boiler, House Mover, and Loafer. Many of the South's fighters were farmers, but their lists also include Gentleman, Shoemaker, Student, Convict, and Rogue.

Did all soldiers volunteer?
No, the South passed America's first national draft law in April 1862, requiring all white males between 18 and 35 to serve for three years. In March 1863, the North conscripted all able-bodied males age between 20 and 45 (single) and 20 and 35 (married).

What famous Americans avoided the fighting?
Grover Cleveland, who later became President, hired a substitute. The famous business tycoon J.D. Rockefeller claimed to have hired 30 different substitutes.

Who were the tallest soldiers?
David Van Buskirk, a 6 ft 11 in-(2.1 m-) soldier captured in 1862 and exhibited as the "Biggest Yankee in the World," enjoyed telling President Davis that he had six sisters taller than himself. In the Southern corner was Texan Private Henry Thruston, who measured 7 ft 7 in (2.3 m).

13

Did all the soldiers use the same weapons?

N O, VOLUNTEERS ARRIVED WITH ALL KINDS OF WEAPONS, AND BOTH governments also bought poor firearms from abroad. They were known as "pumpkin slingers" because they were so heavy and clumsy, and "mules" because they had a terrible "kick", or recoil.

How was the war similar to World War I?

As the war dragged on, regiments defended their positions by digging trenches and protecting them with wire entanglements, tripwires, earthworks, and sharpened stakes. They invented many of the tactics and defenses used in World War I.

Why did soldiers use bayonets as candlesticks?

Of all the wounds suffered in the Civil War, 94 percent were caused by bullets. Soldiers threw their bayonets away as useless, or drove them into the walls of their huts and used them as candlesticks.

Union soldiers setting up a cannon.

How did firearms develop during the Civil War?

Before the war, soldiers fired round balls from flintlock muskets with smooth barrels. These were difficult to load and usually missed their target. General Grant said the enemy could "fire at you all day without you ever finding it out." They were quickly replaced by rifles with grooves cut into the barrels, which fired pointed bullets. These were easier to load, more powerful, and deadly accurate. Both sides now had the firepower to inflict terrible casualties.

What other inventions were used in the fighting?

A primitive flame-thrower was used by one General Butler. And camouflage must have been used, as Confederate troops wrote about shooting down "moving bushes."

Who threw watermelons?
The Dictator was the name given to a giant 17,000-pound mortar, as tall as a man, which lobbed iron cannonballs the size of watermelons on to the enemy lines. Artillerymen chalked their names and addresses on these missiles before firing them.

Was germ warfare ever used?
No, but it was suggested. A Louisiana slave owner named R. Barrow wrote to Congress with a plan to send the corpse of a man who had died from yellow fever into New Orleans to start an epidemic there.

Who invented the land mine?

GENERAL GABRIEL RAINS OF NORTH CAROLINA DEVELOPED LAND mines for the South, which he called "land torpedoes." They were set off by pressure or tripwires. General Sherman forced Confederate soldiers to dig up these "infernal machines."

Confederate soldiers with a battery of cannons.

Who first used a machine gun?
In 1862. The North first used their "Union repeating gun" in a skirmish near Harper's Ferry. It was known as a "coffee mill gun" because it was operated by turning a crank, which operated a revolving cylinder. The Confederates invented their own machine gun, called the Williams gun, and claimed to have first inflicted casualties with it at Seven Pines in May 1862.

New York Herald correspondents sketched and wrote notes on what they saw on the battlefield.

Corresponder outside the N Herald wagon

Who had the best horses?
At the beginning of the war, troops from the rural South were much the better cavalry. They were allowed to ride their own thoroughbreds, and came from a tradition of excellent cavalrymen.

What brought the war to the people back home?
For the first time, photographers stumbled on to battlegrounds with their heavy equipment and asked soldiers to remain still while their photos were taken. The most famous photographer was New York's Mathew B. Brady. He shocked New York City in 1862 with an exhibition of photos of the dead. One visitor noted: "If he has not brought bodies and laid them in our dooryards, he has done something very like it."

Who invented a horseshoe machine?
The Union had much better technology. They invented a horseshoe machine that could produce 60 horseshoes a minute. As the South's mounts and equipment became exhausted, the North's improved.

Who blew up bridges?

IN REVENGE FOR THE MANY ATTACKS ON HIS TRANSPORT SYSTEM, HAUPT wrote an instruction manual showing Union troops how to destroy Confederate railroads. He also invented the tools for the job: a rail-bending "hook" and a "torpedo" for blowing up bridges.

Who traveled by rail?
The North, which had a more advanced rail system, was able to transport its troops, heavy guns, and supplies from east to west much more quickly than the South. For many soldiers, the journey to the front was their first experience of a train journey.

What went up in the air to spy on the enemy?

HOT AIR BALLOONS WERE USED TO SPY ON ENEMY POSITIONS. THEY WERE pioneered by showman Thaddeus Lowe, who founded the U.S. Balloon Corps after demonstrating a balloon to the president. From 300 ft (92 m), the pilot could help his gunners to aim, or relay details of enemy troop positions by telegraph. One balloon flew from the barge *George Washington Parke Custis*—making the barge the world's first aircraft carrier.

Who used telescopes, flashlights, and telegraph?

Albert J. Myer founded the U.S. Army Signal Corps. He trained units of men to use telescopes, flags, flashlights and the recent invention of the telegraph to set up a communications network for the North. By the end of the war, the vast army was linked with thousands of miles of telegraph wire.

Who built rubber boats for spies?

Brigadier General Herman Haupt was the North's transportation chief. His engineering genius masterminded the Union's excellent railroad system. He also built fortified and portable bridges, and portable rubber boats for spies. When Confederates sabotaged the North's railroads, Haupt's Construction Corps repaired them with incredible speed.

Who were the spies?

Spies operated on both sides. The Union had a famous secret agent named Timothy Webster, who was hanged in 1862 for spying. The Confederates had a famous woman spy called Belle Boyd, who was known as the Siren of the Shenandoah.

Who was Allan Pinkerton?

Pinkerton had famously set up one of the first private detective agencies in 1850. After the war started, he escorted Lincoln to his inauguration and started a "secret service" for the Union.

The railroad was very new to the United States during the Civil War.

The *St. Louis* was the first ironclad gunboat built in the United States.

What were "ironclads"?

The "ironclads" were a new type of ship that looked more like submarines. They had steam-driven propellers and were covered in armor plating. The first was the South's *Merrimac*, an old frigate covered with flattened railroad tracks. She sunk three of the North's ships on March 8, 1862. The following day she battled with the North's own ironclad *Monitor* in the first sea battle between these strange craft. This is the point in history where traditional wooden warships began to be replaced by modern battleships.

Who would not surrender?
Under the command of Captain James Iredell Waddell, the Confederate ship *Shenandoah* roamed the Atlantic Ocean sinking Union shipping. Waddell ignored messages saying the war was over and continued fighting. He did not surrender until seven months after the South's surrender.

When did a submarine first sink a ship?
On February 17, 1864, the Confederate submarine *Hunley* attacked the Union ship *Housatonic*. The submarine was powered by eight infantrymen operating hand cranks. Her designer Horace L. Hunley had been killed during trial runs of this dangerous device, along with several crew members. The *Hunley* attacked with a "torpedo," which was actually a mine attached to a spear on the submarine's nose. The explosion sunk the ship—but also the submarine.

What snake set out to strangle the South?

"Scott's Anaconda" was the nickname given to the North's naval blockade of the South. It was designed to work like a great snake, strangling the South by cutting off their supplies, and was suggested by General Winfield Scott.

How did Britain pay for the war?

The Geneva Tribunal of Arbitration decided in 1872 that Britain had not remained neutral because it helped built Confederate ships. She had to pay the United States $15.5 million for damages these ships did to the Union navy.

Was the Civil War fought only on land?

No, Union ships blockaded the South and supported their armies from the Mississippi. Confederate raiders fought back by attacking the North's merchant shipping. The North's powerful navy grew to 670 ships, and the South's to 130.

How did the Mississippi River help the North?

By controlling the Mississippi, the North divided the South into two and was able to contain the fighting within a certain area. It could also support and supply its troops by running ships up and down the river.

Who flushed a toilet underwater?

The eccentric but brilliant Swedish engineer John Ericsson designed the first ironclads used by the North. He also invented the screw propeller, revolving gun turrets, an anchor with four flukes (the arrows that stick in the sea-bed), and a flush toilet that worked below the waterline.

Who painted the Civil War in the English Channel?

The great French painter Manet depicted the sinking of the famous Confederate raider *Alabama* by the North's *Kearsage* in the English Channel. Under the command of the brilliant Captain Raphael Semmes, the *Alabama* had gained her fame by defeating 65 Union ships.

Who fired the first torpedo?

IN OCTOBER 1862, THE SOUTH CREATED THE TORPEDO SERVICE. IT WAS responsible for laying the mines—then called "torpedoes" —in harbors and rivers, which sank 43 Union ships. The most common "Rains" torpedoes (named after their inventor) were made from beer kegs.

Submarines were very dangerous and unsophisticated vessels. Many men were killed in them.

A makeshift church houses a Catholic service.

The church tried to support the soldiers and prevent them from spending too much time gambling and drinking. There were regular services.

Which regiment hoped to put their feet up?

The Union's 7th New York Unit, which contained fashion-conscious soldiers from Grammarcy Park, marched off to war with 1,000 velvet-covered footstools.

How were soldiers punished for misbehaving?

When they became bored during lulls in the fighting, soldiers regularly fought, gambled, thieved, and got drunk on whiskies with names like "Bust Skull." Soldiers also deserted, sometimes so that they could receive money for re-enlisting. Punishments were designed to humiliate: having your head shaved, wearing a sign showing your crime, being paraded in a barrel or being sat on an enormous wooden horse. Flogging was illegal, but branding (with a hot iron) was common.

What uniforms did the soldiers wear?

OFFICIALLY, THE SOUTH WORE GRAY AND THE NORTH WORE BLUE. BUT this was a war of amateur soldiers, who reported for duty in uniforms ranging from kilts to busbies. One Southern captain fought in jaguar-skin trousers with matching holsters!

Camp life could be very boring, so soldiers played a lot of card games that often involved gambling.

What were soldiers supposed to eat?

Both sides had generous rations at the beginning of the war. The official daily issue for each soldier was 12 oz (300 g) of pork or 1 lb 4 oz (600 g) of beef; 1 lb (500 g) of hardtack or 1 lb 4 oz (600 g) of corn; plus beans, rice, coffee, sugar, salt, and pepper.

Which regiment had the most famous mascot?

The 8th Wisconsin Regiment had an eagle named Old Abe as their mascot. Three of the bearers, who carried Old Abe into battle on a perch, were shot from under him, but he lived to enjoy great fame until 1881.

The mess kitchen was a makeshift wooden building.

What were "worm castles"?

THE BISCUITS CALLED "HARDTACK," WHICH WERE THE SOLDIERS' STAPLE DIET.

Soldiers called them "worm castles" because they became infested with maggots and weevils in storage. They were also known as "teeth-dullers" and "sheet-iron crackers" because they were so hard you had to soak them in coffee or break them with a rifle butt. Hardtack was so maggoty that one soldier said: "All the fresh meat we had came in the hard bread."

How could a gun grind coffee?

A few lucky soldiers had coffee-mills built into their rifles. This showed how much coffee was valued. When the Union blockade caused shortages, Rebel soldiers had to drink substitutes made from peanuts and potatoes.

Did the soldiers have enough to eat?

Both sides produced enough to feed their troops, but the South did not have the railroads to transport supplies properly or the salt to preserve it. Starvation at the end of the war caused some Confederate troops to mutiny.

What was "salt horse"?

This was the soldiers' name for the beef they were given, which was pickled with enough salt for it to last two years. One soldier complained that the meat was so bad the buzzards would not eat it.

Fort Sumter

What happened at Fort Sumter?

Confederate artillery started bombarding the Union's Fort Sumter, near Charleston Harbor on April 12, 1861. The following day, the fort commander surrendered. More importantly, the attack had signaled the start of the war.

What was the bloodiest day of the war?

The forces of General Lee and General McClellan met at Antietam Creek, near the town of Sharpsburg. In the single bloodiest day of the war, 10,000 Confederate and 12,000 Union soldiers were killed or wounded.

What was the first big battle?

THE FIRST MAJOR ENGAGEMENT OF THE WAR TOOK PLACE ON JULY 21, 1861,

at Bull Run. The glory of war that some troops had imagined became a horrific reality. A Union officer said of his troops: "They seemed to be paralyzed, standing with their eyes and mouths wide open, and did not seem to hear me." The Union suffered a surprise defeat, and realized that a quick victory would not be theirs.

Who panicked at Bull Run?

Amazingly, the battle was watched by sightseers, including some congressmen, who had traveled down in buggies from Washington. Dressed in their fine clothes, they set up their picnics near the battlefield so they could watch the 75,000 troops do battle. When the Union forces started their retreat, these panicking spectators helped turn it into a rout that almost reached Washington.

Generals and commanders often viewed the battles from a safe distance.

How did Thomas J. Jackson become known as "Stonewall"?

General Jackson became Lee's right-hand man in the war. At Bull Run, a Confederate general rallied his troops by pointing at Jackson and crying: "There stands Jackson like a stone wall! Rally behind the Virginians!"

What did it mean to "see the elephant"?

It was the troops' nickname for fighting the enemy for the first time. It must have been a terrifying experience. The phrase was taken from farm boys, who expressed wonder at "seeing the elephant" after visiting the circus for the first time.

Who was Elmer E. Ellsworth?

The famous 24-year-old colonel was the first officer to die in the war. He led the first Union troops to go South. When he was shot by an innkeeper while taking down a Confederate flag in Alexandria, the North was outraged.

What famous battles were fought in the first part of the war?

Important battles and campaigns included Bull Run (July 16, 1861), the Shenandoah Valley Campaign (December 1861 to June 1862), the Seven Days' Battles (June 25 to July 1, 1862), Antietam Creek (September 17, 1862), Fredericksburg (December 13, 1862), and Chancellorsville (May 2, 1862).

"Stonewall" Jackson was seen as a brave leader of men.

Who killed "Stonewall" Jackson?

AT THE BATTLE OF CHANCELLORSVILLE, JACKSON WAS MISTAKENLY SHOT BY his own troops. He had an arm amputated and died—like many soldiers—from illness caused by his wounds.

What did Confederate troops hope to capture at Honey Springs?

Slaves. The Confederates took slave shackles with them into battle at Honey Springs on July 17th, 1863, because they were fighting against black Union troops whom they expected to capture. In fact, this battle in Indian Territory was won by the 1st Kansas Colored Volunteers.

23

The Gettysburg address is still known as one of the greatest speeches of all time.

What is the Gettysburg Address?
So many men died at Gettysburg that a cemetery covering 17 acres was created there. When Lincoln dedicated it on November 19, 1863, he made the Gettysburg Address—one of the most famous speeches in American history.

What was Pickett's charge?
12,000 infantrymen slowly advanced in a straight line under General George Pickett right into the mouths of the Union artillery. As they marched forward, the Union artillery cut them down in their thousands. It made a noise "strange and terrible, a sound that came from thousands of human throats ... like a vast mournful roar." When Pickett was asked to reorganize his division, he replied: "General Lee, I have no division now."

Three Confederate soldiers, captured during the battle of Gettysburg.

What was the Battle of Gettysburg?

THE MOST FAMOUS BATTLE EVER FOUGHT ON AMERICAN SOIL. AN ARMY OF 75,000 Confederate soldiers attacked 87,000 entrenched Union troops at the market town of Gettysburg, Pennsylvania, from July 1 to 3, 1863. When the South's charge on the final day was cut down, any hope for a Confederate victory in the war was lost.

Why did the men of Pickett's charge stop advancing?

Even as the cannonballs flew among them, they stopped to make sure that their line was straight. One of the Union soldiers mumbled in horrified disbelief: "My God! They're dressing the line."

Who were the commanding officers at Gettysburg?

The Union forces were commanded by General George Meade. During the battle he was said to be "quick, bold, cheerful, and hopeful." The Confederates were commanded by Robert E. Lee, who repeated sadly after Pickett's charge: "It's all my fault."

How many soldiers died at Gettysburg?

Lee lost 28,000 men, while Meade lost 23,000. Some regiments were virtually wiped out. The 26th North Carolina Infantry lost 708 dead and wounded out of 800 men.

Who died without firing a shot?

SOME OF THE SOLDIERS AT GETTYSBURG WERE COMPLETELY UNTRAINED and had never even fired a rifle in action. After the battle, many single-shot rifles were found stuffed with up to 10 charges. Their owners had kept reloading them without ever managing to fire them.

Who put his own bones in a museum?

Major General Daniel Sickles was a Union general who was struck by a cannonball at Gettysburg. His leg had to be amputated, and he instructed the bones to be sent to the Army Medical Museum, where he visited them for many years.

What famous battles were fought in the later part of the war?

Famous engagements and campaigns included the capture of Vicksburg (July 1, 1863), Chickamauga (September 19—20, 1863), the Battle of the Wilderness (May 5—6, 1864), and the Siege of Petersburg (June 1864—April 1865).

General Lee was a brilliant leader and battle tactician.

What happened to captured soldiers?

Many captured soldiers on both sides were kept in terrible prison camps. Andersonville Prison in Georgia was the worst of these. More than one in three of the Union soldiers held there died from starvation and disease, a total of some 13,000 men. Photographs taken of prisoners, who somehow survived show the terrible effects, of starvation. Former inmates of one prison weighed less than 100 lb (45 kg).

Who was Henry Wirz?

Captain Henry Wirz was the Swiss commander of the prison at Andersonville. The press named him the "Andersonville Savage," and after a show trial he was found guilty of war crimes and hanged in front of a huge crowd.

How many soldiers died in prison?

About 194,000 Union soldiers were held prisoner, and 30,000 of them died. Some 214,000 Confederate soldiers were held in prison camps in the North, where 26,000 died.

Where did General Lee surrender?

AT 3:00 P.M. ON PALM SUNDAY, APRIL 9, 1865, LEE SIGNED the surrender at the courthouse in Appomattox, Virginia. Under the terms agreed with General Grant, all Confederate soldiers could return home without facing trial for treason. Lee also made a special request that those cavalrymen with their own horses might be allowed to take them back to their homes.

What is Providence Spring?

A T ANDERSONVILLE, THE DRINKING WATER WAS FILTHY. BUT IN

August 1864, after a rainstorm, a spring of pure, clean water bubbled up from the ground. The prisoners, believing it was a sign that God had not forgotten them, called it Providence Spring. It still flows today.

What vandal led the "March to the Sea"?
At the end of 1864, the North's Major General William Tecumseh Sherman led his troops through Georgia from Atlanta to the coast. The "Vandal Chief" used a new form of warfare, burning or seizing property to break the will of the civilian population.

How many battles were there?
The war lasted for 1,489 days, from the capture of Fort Sumter on April 12, 1861, until the last battle at Palmito Ranch on May 12, 1865 (Lee was not the last to surrender). In this time there were over 10,000 engagements, big and small, between the two sides.

What happened to the armies after the Confederates surrendered?
After turning in their arms, Confederate soldiers were simply left to make their own way home. The roads were soon crowded with them. Ships and trains carried the Union troops to their home states, where they were paid and discharged.

What horror happened on board *The Sultana*?
The Sultana was a paddle steamer designed to carry 370 passengers. On April 24, 1865, she left Vicksburg with 2,000 freed Union prisoners aboard. When her boiler exploded, 1,700 men who had survived the horrors of prisoner-of-war camps perished in the inferno.

Confederate soldiers return home.

Clara Barton helped many
wounded soldiers.

What operation was most often performed on the battlefield?

Three out of four operations performed in the field hospitals were amputations. The bullets fired by civil war rifles inflicted terrible damage. Surgeons regarded amputation as the only way to stop disease spreading in badly injured limbs. But their equipment was never sterilized, and it was quite rare for a surgeon to wash his hands or instruments between operations.

Why were casualties so high?

The poor soldiers in the civil war were fighting a battle at the worst point in history. Advances in weapons meant that the ability to kill and wound had suddenly increased. But the surgeon's ability to mend and heal had not yet entered the modern age.

How did smugglers get quinine and morphine to their troops?

Women and children sometimes carried dolls from the North to the South. In the hollow heads and bodies were precious medical supplies.

Who was Clara Barton?

SHE WAS A NEW ENGLAND WOMAN WHO WORKED IN A PATENT office. She placed an advert in a newspaper asking for medical supplies, then carried them to the battlefield. There she provided a soup kitchen and offered bandages and medicine to the wounded. After the war, in 1881, she founded the American Red Cross. A senator said: "She has the talent of a statesman, the command of a general, and the heart and hand of a woman."

Hospitals were often makeshift and unhygienic.

Which side had the best medical services?

All the major pharmacies were located in the North. Two government laboratories were set up in 1863, employing chemists and 350 workers to make medicines and pills.

Amputations were common, but many died from infected wounds as a result of the operation.

How many soldiers died in the Civil War?

IN THE CIVIL WAR, 620,000 MEN LOST THEIR LIVES, WHICH IS MORE than in all the United State's other wars combined. Of these, 60 percent died from disease. As a comparison, in World War II, 405,000 American troops lost their lives.

What were hospital standards like in 1861?

Doctors had no antibiotics, no understanding of bacteria or sterilization, and no knowledge of the connection between filthy water and disease. If they survived their wounds, patients were likely to die from typhoid, dysentery, or pneumonia.

What did Louisa May Alcott say about hospitals?

The famous author of *Little Women*, who worked as a Union nurse in the war, wrote: "A more perfect pestilence box than this I never saw—cold, damp, dirty, full of vile odors from wounds, kitchens, and stables."

What drugs were successful?

To treat malaria, doctors had quinine, which is still used for that purpose today. Opium was an effective painkiller, but soldiers became addicted to it. Chloroform was used as an anaesthetic.

Lincoln was shot in this box at Ford's theater.

What did John Wilkes Booth do at the theater?

On the evening of Good Friday, April 14, 1865, the actor rushed into Lincoln's box at Ford's Theater and fired a single pistol shot into the president's head. He then leapt from the box, breaking his leg but still managing to escape. Lincoln died the following morning. Booth was later killed. Strangely, Booth had been present at the hanging of John Brown just before the war began.

Why did Lincoln not want to go to the theater?

He had had a clear dream in which he foresaw his own death. In this dream, which he recounted to his wife, he saw himself lying in his coffin.

When did the Civil War end slavery?

OFFICIALLY, ACCORDING TO THE EMANCIPATION Proclamation that Lincoln had made during the war, it ended on January 1, 1863. Actually, votes for blacks were first put into force in the South in 1867.

Payne, one of Booth's associates was arrested for the murder of Lincoln.